Savage Charm
Ahmed Elbeshlawy
Proverse Hong Kong
2019

About the cover image by the poet
The photograph was taken at Causeway Bay at the pedestrian crossing in front of the Sogo department store. Since *Savage Charm* is inspired by Hong Kong – a transitional place which seems to perpetuate the state of transition – crossing – or in fact, the impossibility of crossing – seems to be at the heart of the book. I have always thought of Hong Kong as a crossing from one place to another, but I have never moved from the state of crossing itself; unable to move forward to a new world or to go back to an old one. Crossing can also be a crossing between cultures which, in the case of Hong Kong, still remains largely thwarted.

SAVAGE CHARM is autobiographical at its core, but also unsentimental, unapologetic, and rigorous in its exploration of such related concepts as self-knowledge, fictional identity, the city, the writing of exile, belief, religion, and the modern subject. The poet brings his distinctive voice to cosmopolitan Hong Kong's English poetic scene with this volume which records his personal experience of the city in the subtlest of ways. Though deeply personal, the poems have a gutsy impersonal touch and a distinctive social tinge. *Savage Charm* is both poetic and philosophical.

AHMED ELBESHLAWY is a scholar of comparative literature. He is author of *Twenty Five Meditations on Writing and Subjectivity* (2019), *Woman in Lars von Trier's Cinema* (2016), *America in Literature and Film* (2011), and various articles and book chapters in *The Palgrave Handbook of Literature and the City* (2016), *Sexuality and Culture* (2014), *The Comparatist* (2008), *Scope* (2008), and *fe/male bodies* (2005, 2006).

Having come to Hong Kong in 1995 with a background in English Studies, he has become used to thinking comparatively across disciplines, literatures, and cultures. He is interested in all aspects of English literature and literary and cultural theories. He started writing English poems more or less secretly at the age of 15 in Egypt, but never read them – not even to his closest acquaintances – until the age of forty in Hong Kong. He always thought – still thinks – that poetry is a "dangerous domain" and that "academic writing is much safer". Writing poetry, to him, is the "ultimate surrender of the self to the other".

Ahmed works at the Consulate-General of the United Arab Emirates in Hong Kong. He teaches occasionally at HKU SPACE where his courses cover a range of topics from Greek, Renaissance, modernist and contemporary literature to critical film and art analysis.

SAVAGE CHARM

Ahmed Elbeshlawy

Proverse Hong Kong

Savage Charm
By Ahmed Elbeshlawy
ISBN: 978-988-8491-67-4
1st edition published in paperback in Hong Kong
by Proverse Hong Kong, P.O. Box 259, Tung Chung Post Office,
Lantau, NT, Hong Kong SAR, China.
Email: proverse@netvigator.com; Web: www.proversepublishing.com
Copyright © Proverse Hong Kong, 2019.

Distribution (Hong Kong and worldwide)
The Chinese University Press of Hong Kong,
The Chinese University of Hong Kong,
Shatin, New Territories, Hong Kong SAR.
Email: cup@cuhk.edu.hk; Web: www.cup.cuhk.edu.hk

Distribution (United Kingdom)
Stephen Inman, Worcester, UK

The right of Ahmed Elbeshlawy to be identified
as the author of this work
has been asserted by him in accordance with
the Copyright, Designs and Patents Act 1988.

Cover image by Ahmed Elbeshlawy
Cover design by Artist Hong Kong.

British Library Cataloguing in Publication Data
A catalogue record is available
from the British Library

Preface

How many Hong Kongs are there? How many languages in it? How many modes of expression? This volume of poetry, *Savage Charm*, is a reminder that there are more than you think, despite efforts to homogenise it, whether in terms of a Chinese city, or in terms of making it a dream-city of Western capitalism. If asked to find a model for this poetry of uprootedness and a strange sense of alienation, it would be Baudelaire's *Les Fleurs du Mal* (1857), which equally writes about the poet's relationships with women, as symptomatic of a malaise and boredom (*ennui*) the poet feels in modernity, but nonetheless includes a section on Paris in the middle, 'Tableaux Parisiens'. Ahmed Elbeshlawy does something similar. He puts 'The City' into the midst of sections whose primary subjects are women and relationships, or their lack. Hong Kong, as an exemplar of so many cities in modernity, but still, in its colonialism and neo-colonialism, attempting to be other cities (North American particularly), becomes the subject of these poems, written by a third voice which is neither Chinese nor conventionally Western, and which shows how many 'alternative histories' are to be read within it. Baudelaire, one of the great theorists of modern city-life, in verse and in prose, has influenced these poems, giving character to them as they try to think about 'modernity': its isolating effects, whether in a lift or the MTR; its presence as a text, well caught in the poem 'Advertisements'; its attempted narcissism with its selfie-sticks; and its draining of lived experience and memory.

If I mention Baudelaire, that is because this poetry has a wide range of references: its author is aware of the French psychoanalyst Jacques Lacan, so controversially discussed by Slavoj Žižek, and so brought into relationship with film-theory. The most obviously Lacanian poem here is 'Believer', but Lacan is present throughout the complex responses to feminism here (and the author has written a fine monograph on *Women in Lars Von Trier's Cinema*). One poem, ('Eye'), concentrates on Georges Bataille's *The Story of the Eye*, a novella critiquing the Cartesian sense of the eye as separating subject and object, in the way I look at you: distancing you, making you an object. And other authors too: Shakespeare, Ibsen, Brecht, feed these poems very profitably, making them not merely personal, but ways of thinking about the relationships of men and women (and men-men, in 'Aufidius after the Death of Martius') in modern urban life.

Elbeshlawy says in his Introduction that he does not know what poetry is, but what emerges in this collection is that poetry cannot be one thing; there is an astonishing play of rhythms, rhymes, and half-rhymes, different metres and half-metres, different lengths of poem, and different forms, so that anyone coming to them will be impressed by writing which does not settle down into one thing, but which ranges and experiments, its English, punning and playful, being neither conventionally poetic, nor allowing the reader to relax: everything here demands the sharpest attention.

Jeremy Tambling
Professor of English
Warsaw University of Social Sciences and Humanities

for R

Contents

Preface by Jeremy Tambling   5
Introduction by the Author   13

IMPERFECTIONS

The Untranslatable   23
A Chase to Death   24
The Selfie   25
It Isn't Complete Just Yet   26
Hell Dwellers   28
It Isn't Your Mind   29
Academia   31
Location   32
Words   33
Truth   34
Poem   35
Eye   36
No   38
A forgotten Sinner   40
Imperfections   42
Proximity   43

THE CITY

Human Resources   47
To a Chinese Poet Whom I Knew   48
Commuting   50
The Selfie Stick   51
Hongkonger   52
Hongkonger in the MTR   53
Containers   54
Ode to a Cheongsam   55
Brief Encounters I   57
Brief Encounters II   58
Receptions and Conferences   59

Amusement   60
Old Hongkonger   61
A Hong Kong Artist   62
Ludic Democracy   63
Capitalist Democracy   64
Spikes   65
Advertisements   66
Chinese Café, Hong Kong in 1995   67
A Hong Kong Winter   68
The Death of Master Wu Yong Deren, also known as   69
Mr Yogurt, in the Year 2047
The City of Screens   71
The Forbidden City   73
Numbered   75
I Dreamt of a Mask   77
Heather   79
A Fulfilled Promise   81

WOMAN

Plain Woman   85
Sign   87
Mother   88
Anxiety   89
She   90
Distraction   92
Inspiration   93
The Unattainable One   94
Flowers   95
Believer   96
The Other Woman   97
Hymen   99
Aria   101
Mark   103
The Goddess of Chaos Talks to Equus   104

ALTERNATIVE HISTORIES

Henry VIII in His Stables on the 28th of January 1547 — 107

Two Egyptian Lovers, Tel-el-Amarna in 1327 B.C. — 108

Potiphar's Wife Visiting Joseph in Jail — 110

A Group of Christian Monks, Alexandria in 415 A.D. — 111

Aufidius after the Death of Martius — 112

The Shrewdness of Odysseus — 113

Dr. Rank's Final Words to Torvald — 115

Abraham's Wife — 116

Baal Coming to Thebes — 117

Horatio after Hamlet's Death — 119

Bertha Talking to Herself in the Attic — 120

Poe, Baltimore on the 3rd of October 1849 — 122

Burying Ishmael — 123

Bibliography and Filmography — 127

Advance Comments — 131

Notes — 132

Introduction

This collection of poems is mainly inspired by my life in Hong Kong – a centre of conglomerates as it were to which I always personally felt it impossible to belong in spite of the fact that I have lived half of my life in it. I came to Hong Kong on Christmas Eve in 1994 with no real intention to stay in it for long. The casualness of coming to the city twenty-four years ago only seems to me to swell the magnitude of that event today. I made many friends in the city. I was in and out of several love affairs. Yet, I always felt utterly and inexplicably lonely. It is this uncanny feeling of solitude in a city which seems to impose on one a sense of perpetual festivity that preceded every poem in this volume. As someone invested in literary and cultural studies almost all of my life in Hong Kong, writing, eventually, seems to me to have become the ultimate end towards which everything else gravitated. Working, exercising, dining, wining, smoking, praying, making money and making love finally became *activities* that precede and lead to the only real *act*.

I cannot pretend that I am satisfied with any definition of poetry. I do not know what it is. And, I have serious doubts about those who say that they do. I do believe though that poetry can never be explained adequately. Not that the poems included in this volume call for any explanation, as, I think, most of them are quite direct, accessible, and even lacking in literary guile. Most of the poems were in fact written before this writer became increasingly interested in academic writing and doctrinaire literature. It is left to the reader to decide for himself/herself what is obviously serious in the poems and what can perhaps be described in one way or another as campy or making light of what is in fact taken seriously. Some of the poems are about Hong Kong in a quite direct manner. However, it wouldn't be inaccurate to say that *all* of the poems are about Hong Kong in one way or another.

Until now I never wrote any critical or analytical essay about Hong Kong. Somehow I find the city impossible to talk about except in poetic/chaotic terms. The poems included in this volume are chosen from a considerably longer list which remains unpublished, mostly unread by anyone but the writer, and more or less kept in secret. I have to admit that I do not feel safe in the dangerous domain of poetry. Reading my own poems to myself gives me a feeling of nakedness under an intolerable gaze.

With its autobiographical underpinnings, I am afraid this volume of poetry may appear to be more onanistic than anything else. It shouldn't be surprising to state that poetry is, de facto and de jure, the most onanistic form of writing, since most people think of it as too personal and self-reflexive. However, I do believe that the survival of the form since ancient times to the present moment does indicate that poetry has always found its way to play aesthetics against politics and vice versa; in other words, to display gutsy social, political, or cultural tinges from time to time through nothing but personal experience. Not to mention that onanism itself can be politicized if seen as a threat to the sexual relationship in the sense of subordinating instead of supplementing it. I believe that most readers will be able to see beyond the personal in the poems.

Based on a preliminary long discussion between myself and my publisher's editor, who generously provided me with invaluable expert advice and insight, a few points must be made clear in order to avoid some pitfalls regarding possible religious sensitivities. This collection of poems is not intended to be offensive in any way to any religion. The reader will come across a number of Christian and Muslim allusions as well as the word "God" on many occasions. In none of these instances does the writer mean to display any blasphemous tendencies. In fact, what may appear to be blasphemous on the surface may be quite the opposite if looked at from a different angle. Let me however start from the notion of blasphemy itself which sometimes gets confused with atheism – not that this writer advocates either.

Blasphemy, unlike atheism, can only exist when a group of people claim in an absolute manner and unshaken confidence that their worldview and eschatological belief necessarily mirror the divine view of God and His intentions. The seed of blasphemy cannot be sown in a world of discursive disagreement with the other that is *necessarily* coupled with self-doubt. In other words, where people disagree over the desire of God, the nature of God, or indeed the existence of God, acknowledging at once an ever-present margin of fallibility in their own views, there can be no room for blasphemy. The next step on the road to planting blasphemy is blocking the ears completely to the view of the other. The final step is incriminating the view of the other. E. M. Forster held a view that "the idea that one religion is false and another true is essentially Christian" (*Alexandria,* 20). If Forster is correct then, clearly, the Christian idea found its way easily to Muslim thought too, until it finally reached its ugliest form in modern Islamic fundamentalism.

God, in the language of institutionalized religion, is God in language or God *of* language. That is why it can be understood from Jacques Lacan's analysis of the moral law that the history of religion is marked by a movement from the imaginary to the symbolic; in other words, from gods and goddesses that can be seen to the one male God who cannot be seen but is manifested only in language. The second commandment, "Thou shalt not make unto thee any graven image" (*The Bible*, Exodus 20:4), "excludes not only every cult, but also every image, every representation of what is in heaven, on earth, or in the void"; it eliminates the "function of the imaginary" and establishes a "relation to the symbolic" in the sense of "speech" (Lacan, *Ethics* 81). Civilization starts with a "primordial law" that "superimposes the reign of culture over the reign of nature"

(*Écrits: The First Complete Edition* 229). It also clearly imposes the reign of man over woman.

This writer believes that it is only in this particular sense that "God" can and indeed is referred to in the language of institutionalized religion. And, it is in the same specific sense that "God" is referred to in some of the poems in this volume. A true belief in God, on the other hand, necessitates taking Him out of religious discourse altogether; indeed, out of language. And, since language is the precondition of thought, a true believer must accept that God, in the Real, cannot be articulated or talked about except in terms of complete mystery. Not knowing what God exactly is or what He wants is, to this writer, a sign of true belief. The foreclosure of God in the real – a procedure that is performed most notably by the world's major monotheistic religions through ideating God as a father, or as a human being, or indeed through bestowing godly attributes on human beings – creates at once God in language; the God of cultural interpretations. And it is precisely the God of cultural interpretations in whose name all of the past and present atrocities of religion have been committed. For "within the space of language, we 'regress' to the level of Being" (Žižek, *Interrogating the Real* 182). Once God exists in language, He *is*, but that in itself is necessarily a regression. This is the "God" referred to in the poems.

In this sense, affirming the presence of God in language is paradoxically a sign of *disbelief* in God's existence. True believers must die in doubt, not in entire belief, because belief loses its very meaning if its ultimate dimension is revealed. Belief, *by its very definition*, must "presuppose in its basis that the ultimate dimension that it has to reveal is strictly correlative with the moment when its meaning is about to fade away" (Lacan, *Four Fundamental Concepts* 238). Therefore, the discourse – any discourse – which makes it its business to completely obliterate human doubt, obliterates human belief with it.

God, in the Real, has none of the attributes given to him in the language of religion(s). He is a Lévinasian God. He is:

> other than the other [*autre* qu'autrui], other otherwise, other with an alterity prior to the alterity of the other, prior to the ethical bond with another and different from every neighbor, transcendent to the point of absence, to the point of a possible confusion with the stirring of the *there is* . (Lévinas, *Collected Philosophical Papers* 165–6)

With that said – and in order not to be mistaken for a feminist, even though I do admire many feminists – the typical feminist critique of religious discourse, which suggests that it is man who invented God in his own male image or, more interestingly, that "patriarchy attacked and finally managed to overthrow the ancient established religions of the Mother Goddess, who preceded male gods in every mythology in the world" (Walker 268), seems to repress the fact that this is a fight over nothing but a master signifier in language. Over and above both the religious discourse and the feminist critique of it, perhaps male and female cooperated and in a way even conspired to make God male; man wanted to make him male in his own image to establish some sort of symbolic authority over woman, and woman, with a more complicated and ambitious intention, wanted to make God male in order to complete the circuit and render God, as his male inventor, a creation of language and no more. Put another way, man invented an ideology and woman subverted it by what Žižek refers to as the literal identification with ideology. For "*stepping out of (what we experience as) ideology is the very form of our enslavement to it*" (*Žižek Reader* 60). Subverting ideology, on the other hand, can be achieved by nothing except a total and literal identification with its mandates. Žižek gives an example from Heinrich von Kleist's hero in the novella, *Michael Kohlhaas: From an Old Chronicle*, in which the hero identifies himself completely with law and justice to the very limits of overthrowing both in the process (*Did Somebody Say* 32-4).

It can be argued thus that while man historically abstracted himself as God, as can be evidenced in the discourse of religion, woman abstracted the abstraction itself. She did not really try to revise or critique the religious discourse and its male God; she took man's ideological invention as it is and pushed it even further to the very limits of the completely unbelievable. It is an affirmation and a fundamental destabilization of religious discourse at once. Thus, while a feminist critique of the religious discourse works against the grain, revealing its male-oriented foundations, it does not seem to the present writer to be an effective way to destabilize that discourse or the persistence of its framing of the feminine as subaltern in texts that are extremely judicious and soggy with masculine stresses.

Just as avoiding feminism, the present writer would also like to avoid being mistaken for what is quite prevalent in Hong Kong and elsewhere and which goes under the ridiculous postmodern banner of being a 'free thinker'. For the contemporary free thinker seems to me to know neither the religious discourses nor the atheist discourses of the true free thinkers of the past or the present. (S)he won't go to the trouble of making close acquaintance with Yahweh, Christ, or Allah. (S)he definitely won't go to the trouble of understanding what Nietzsche meant by "God is dead" (*The Gay Science* 109, 120 & 199 and *Thus Spoke Zarathustra* 13 & 73), what Freud meant by the "intimate connection between the father-complex and belief in God" (*Art and Literature* 216), what Lacan meant by "*God is unconscious*" (*The Four Fundamental Concepts* 59), what Derrida meant by God as "wholly other", therefore, like "everyone else [...] inaccessible, solitary, transcendent, nonmanifest, originarily nonpresent to my *ego*", just as "my neighbor or my loved ones [...] are as inaccessible to me, as secret and transcendent as Yahweh" (*The Gift of Death* 78). In fact, the present-day free thinker, who is more often than not a yuppie dweller of a cosmopolitan, capitalist, and multicultural city, like Hong Kong for example, is pushed by all means to think freely in order to pose his own big Other in the most pragmatic way possible, that is to say, pushed by all means to mistake politics for 'free thinking'.

(S)he is made to believe that (s)he has been raised by society to be an acutely apolitical, liberal, and non-ideological free thinker while, as a matter of fact, his/her approach to everything and everyone always betrays his/her ultimately ideological and politically correct disposition. In other words, the present day common idea of free thinking is in its essence nothing but what Adorno, back in 1950, called a "pragmatization of politics" which "hides the conviction that there is no objective truth in politics", that "every individual, may behave as [he] likes and that the only thing that counts is success". The crux of the matter is that Adorno believed that "it is precisely this pragmatization of politics which ultimately defines fascist philosophy" (*The Authoritarian Personality* 726). Fascist philosophy is that of a man or a woman who measures everything happening in the present with a pragmatic eye on what he or she counts as a successful final material gain in the future, and who remains totally apathetic to everything else that falls outside the frame of this economy.

To Adorno, this "pragmatization of politics" goes perfectly with the use of religion as a "practical aid in the mental hygiene of the individual" or as merely "something "to hold on to"". In such a case, religion seems to have everything to do with what Adorno calls the "abstract belief in power" (734-738). Mariah Carey's 1998 song, *When You Believe*, which is used as a sound track accompanying the great exodus of the Jews out of Egypt in Brenda Chapman's, Steve Hickner's and Simon Well's *The Prince of Egypt* – which is supposed to be about the belief in the one God of the people of Israel – is a clear manifestation of that, since the word "God" is nowhere to be found in it. In fact the opening line goes: "Many nights we've prayed with no proof anyone could hear", which means that the prayers are not supported by the belief in an existent god, but by the psychological dependence on the hope that someone or something might one day serve as a proof for filling in this gap.

Yet, even when the proof (or the prophet) comes, the main choral line carrying the core message of the song comes along with it with the empty idea of believing as such, without mentioning what it is exactly that one is supposed to believe in: "There can be miracles when you believe". What you believe in is shrewdly left open, partly because it does not sound particularly trendy to insert the word "God" in a modern popular song, but more significantly because what is unconsciously implied here is that what you believe in is ultimately what gives you power, and it can be filled in with anything you deem fit for belief for a practical reason, be it God, money, Hitler, America, ISIS, Trump, etc. The song, thus, even though inserted in a filmic adaptation of a Biblical and Quranic story, is blatantly symptomatic of the position of the contemporary free thinker who believes in whatever gives him/her power; for today's free thinker is as *complacent as the absolute believer*. Both of them do not exercise their intellect over the question of God as a philosophical question. Both are driven by nothing but what they blindly believe in. Both are fascists at their core.

The writer of the poems that you are about to read thus is, simply put, a believer who doubts.

IMPERFECTIONS

The Untranslatable

There are things that I haven't told you yet;
Fundamental things, quite defining ones;
Things that would shake the core of your being
And leave you exhausted, totally spent;
Things that are linguistically savage,
Fervent and vocally traumatizing;
The body gets carved by them unseeing,
As if under sharp invisible knives.
You can't imagine the consequences;
The pleasure and the pain those things can make;
They would lever your inside out wholly
And fill your surroundings with the long ache
Of your long-lost fluids and fragrances;
They would scourge your enemy instantly,
Like a whip dipped in salt for thirty days.
Those are the attributes of the strange things
That, until now, I haven't told you yet,
And, they are untranslatable, thank God!

A Chase to the Death

Well, he vanished from cyberspace,
Nothing came out of him for ninety days,
There must be a reason for this disappearance.
Did he fall in love or is he dead?
If dead, no more can be done or said,
And there is no need for our interference.
If it's love in the way of what he pays
To the almighty cyberspace,
Then he must be brought back at once,
At any cost, in any case.
Check! If necessary, start the chase!

The Selfie

I saw me clicking me
The moment of clicking,
Me was looking at me,
I don't know who clicked whom,
It was like touching my
Own lone genitalia,
I felt the ecstasy
Of me knocking me out,
Smiling at me clicking
Me smiling back at me
At the very moment.

Yet looking back at me
Filled my heart with sadness
And odd melancholy,
And I couldn't show me
Comfortably freely.
How could I possibly
Bare me at this moment
Made of self-made and self-
Inflicted sodomy?

So I invited my
Friends in to fill the frame,
And they stood beside me
Smiling at me clicking
Me smiling back at me.
Finally I can show
Me unashamedly,
Or even tease me and
Display me on a shelf,
For there were witnesses
Who actually saw me
Doing it to myself.

It Isn't Complete Just Yet

Until I am happy with the price tag adorning my chest,
The world continues to be a random throw of dice.
The prostitution of the universe isn't complete yet,
As long as I am still frowning about my own price.

The long days and hours of toiling in subtle slavery
Are not entirely free of erect apprehension,
Nor are they devoid of rebellious innuendos.
The nights, even though so slack, do not lack dreams of
bravery,
And a desire to break free from the suspension
Of all of these ropes hanging out of office windows.

Yes, the evening air seems to be unbelievably stagnant
With a spirit rundown by cold daylight commission,
Yes, the monotonous night seems unnaturally pregnant
With an impotent love that lacks the bite of passion,

But deep down in our hearts, we might still be crowning
fake kings
Without respect, without believing in their power,
Deep down in our hearts, we might still be here just for the
drinks
And the dance and the chance and delight of the hour.

I greet my neighbour – who speaks not – in the morning
with a smile.
He smiles back. We're on the way to our pigeonholes
On the countless rows of display shelves in the market.
We know that the smiles will fade, the frowns will appear
in a while,
As if there is a sure understanding between us
That the prostitution isn't complete – not just yet.

As long as I am still holding this pen and writing this verse

With a care that goes beyond the limits of pleasure,
Then the carefully planned prostitution of the universe
Isn't really complete by any goddam measure.

Hell Dwellers

You do not expect me to love you
In a world that thinks itself so strong
Through abjuring love for good, do you?

We do not hallucinate, it's true,
This is where the briefest song is wrong
And one forgets that the sky is blue.

How can I even know the feeling
If it happens to rise from the grave?
Rise? Have you forgotten where we are?

Our dropped heads don't perceive being,
And even your cave caves in this cave.
Seeking love! Haven't you gone too far?

Dreaming like a Franciscan friar!
We are, after all, hell dwellers, and
Hell dwellers can't but feed the fire.

It Isn't Your Mind

Let us rephrase what we said; it isn't your mind we're
looking for.
Frankly speaking, good friend, it's your rapid running
around in rounds.
We don't mean to offend, you can read and write to your
heart's content,
You can speak for hours if you wish, yell at us, or even
roar.
We do like the poignant performances and the amusing
sounds
Of the overall entertaining class you come to represent.

Shake that imaginary world you talk about with your red
rage,
Wreck havoc with your magic in its exotic nether regions,
Or indeed proceed further and ride your cultural white
winged horse
To fly above our empty little heads and land on the stage,
Present us with the academical dance, test our patience,
You'll find us with neither expectation nor a shred of
remorse.

We will take notes. You can twist thoughts, make paper
boats and linguae bend,
You can commit symbolic suicide every day, we'll clap for
you,
It doesn't really matter whether you believe in what you
say
Or simply chip away at old gods to go with the latest trend.
Yes, you may use 'gay' for 'homosexual' and 'closet' for
the 'loo'.
It's all very interesting, you see, as long as you're kept at
bay.

It isn't your mind we're looking for; it's your mind we're looking for.

Academia

Publish or perish, the institution said;
Words can make you, words can break you;
Cut out of flesh, in sickness or in health,
Publish or perish, publish or perish.

That fisherman was indeed bold;
In the wind, snow, and icy cold,
He played Lear, the tragicomic hero.

That nomad used all his weapons,
Resources, clothes and cattle;
He gave up all – for it can't be a lost battle.
Publish or perish, publish or perish.

That Templar put on his best warrior's attire,
And on the way to Jerusalem, left a trail of fire;
In the name of the Father, the Son, and the Holy Ghost,
Publish or perish.

The sun set on everything in sight,
Yet it shone brightly on the institution of words,
Cleansing daily its ultimate vow –
The maxim that it lives by.

A rainfall of words followed,
Inundating illusionary landscapes;
Publish, publish, publish.

Blinded by the maxim, our heroes couldn't see
The decadence of their situation,
The optical illusion,
Written on every wall of the institution –
"Publish and perish".

Location

Dearest,
There can't be a simple escape
For you or for me where my handprints
Are all over your landscape;
Where my passion is registered
At every turn, upon every curve;
Where fragmented body parts mix with eyes;
Where meaning doesn't operate
And death plays with the liveliest nerve;
Where we exist beyond truths and lies;
Where we cease to exist;
Where dialogue stops and heartbeats grow faster;
Where the night beats daylight
And the body decides to take on the soul
And wreck disaster
Upon its flimsy mansion;
Where the names we go by cease to mean anything
And disappearance becomes our essence –
Our actual presence.

Words

Her threatening messages of final separation
Look like my words of academic retribution;
A terrorist thought on the edge of an abyss;
A peacock's head at the rim of a furnace –
All dwellers of naught, readers of what to miss
In the imagined aftershock of the imagined breakup,
Written with invisible ink, paving the way for my feet
To imprint themselves on her sandy beach yet again,
Clearing the passage for my pen to write the real story
Of my literary addiction to her conservatory –
The school of all arts, the inflamer of the nerves.

Truth

Looking out of her balcony
On one of those stormy days,
She says:

"In Chinese literature, they
Associate women with water",
Then asks me about my culture
Again.
"Do they associate women with rain?"
As if I have a brain
That decodes the devious connotations
Of 'woman'.

Sensing a confusion of meanings,
She wants to know the truth
About my feelings.
Still looking for the 'truth',
While everyone knows what happens
When they catch the truth naked
Under a spotlight against a wall.

Well, my most beloved addiction,
The truth is that
I want you always to be at arm's length;
To be able at any given moment
To pull you nearer and exercise power.
Didn't you want to know the truth?
Didn't you want to catch her naked
Under a spotlight against a wall?

This is it, simply put;
The truth is that
You happen to be the truth.

Poem

You think I am writing a poem.
I think I am writing you.
To my mind you are a poem,
Full of alliteration,
Blissful pits of temptation.

Time and again,
I lose track of time
During hours of hunger.
I hallucinate,
Yet I amazingly maintain
My poem's beautiful rhyme.

I like to think I create a symbol,
While the truth is that
I only bear sticks of incense
Inside your temple.

I like to imagine that the image
Can be contained,
Can be framed,
Can conform to my literary usage,
While the truth is that
Yesterday, I touched your skin,
The surface of the world;
I contemplated my poem's tone.
Today,
I am alone.

Eye

Was it an illusion?
Or did I see that tear
Welling up in your eye?
Confusing notion;
In the middle of my
Delicious perversion,
Attentive penetration,
You cry?!
O Bataille, Bataille,
If only you could see
The 'Story of the Eye'
From where I try
To look and fail
To see –
Fail to cry.
In the beginning
Was the Word.
The word became flesh
And the eye
Was born;
The 'I'
Was born;
The flesh, immediately torn.
The eye explores,
Investigates,
Burns,
Devours.
Love it admits,
But it also splits
'I'.
Replace the eye
With the ear
And you will hear
The Word of the beginning.
It takes a long time

For her, you or me
To understand,
To see
That the eye,
May be,
Wasn't made to look,
O Bataille,
But made to cry.

No

Here she is,
Naked as truth,
With the rosy bud
Gaping and smooth,
Made to please
Her lover's eyes.
Be at ease,
Take your time,
Make love to her,
But, lover, prepare
Yourself to die
At your prime.
This is the law of our town.

Do not let her down,
Make her content,
Let her see you implore
To enter her tent,
Inhale her scent,
Let your hands explore
Every curve
And tenderly test
The size of every bore,
The sensitivity
Of every nerve.
Write your poem,
Enjoy the rhyme,
But, lover, prepare
Yourself to die
At your prime.
This is the law of our town.

We will of course
Excuse you
If you change course,

If you prefer
To abandon her
And outlive your love,
Or your idiocy;
If you are wise enough
To see through the folly
Of chivalry
The wisdom of state and crown,
And live by the law of our town.

***

O hear me,
Magistrates of the law;
Hear me carefully,
For I need not any time
To make my choice.
Hear me God
And let my voice
Come to the notion
Of every soul,
Reach the highest mountain
And the deepest ocean,
The beasts of the jungle,
The birds, and the mice,
All that is basking
In your creation.
I will indeed make love
Neither out of chivalry
Nor even out of love,
But just to say NO
To this town's law.

A Forgotten Sinner

Among those who were forgotten,
A man aged one hundred
At forty-six.
Already consumed and rotten,
Disillusioned, well read,
Who couldn't fix
His own life with words.
There was race
And there was
Sex.
There was prejudice.
There were women
Who constructed his art.
There were men
Whom he admired.
There were lots of
Books.
Some said that he never knew
What he was supposed to do.
Some believed the promises
Of others
That ran on his very tongue
As if they were
his.
He was particularly good
At conveying the promises
Of others.
He was a sinner
Who wasn't even himself.
How to judge a self
That never found itself?
"In the Beginning was the Word."
"This is the Book, free of doubt."
Hell dwellers despise him.
The faithful shun him.

Al-A'raf philosophers disown him.
No one wants him.
Among those who were forgotten,
A man aged one hundred
At forty-six.

Imperfections

It surprises me that you can't see
The power of that stain on your skin;
That you don't seem to realize
This dangerous trap for a lover's wandering gaze.

In your tireless quest for advertised flawlessness,
For perfect symmetries and uninterrupted smoothness,
For the sterile clinical standard image
Of almost everyone in this age of plastic beauties,
Where drinking orange juice and living healthy,
Watching hygiene and never getting sick are sacred duties,
You seem to miss

The importance of imperfections;

The sting of good wine,
The poison in a cup of coffee,
The dark spots most attractive to a lover's kiss,
A protruding bone, a tiny breast,
Eyes with no eyelashes, flat hips or limping legs,
Porous complexion or badly done hair.

And, what goes for the body goes for what you wear;
A broken shoe, a worn out jacket, a torn stocking,
A loose thread at the edge of your skirt
Threatening to unravel it,
A hole on the side of your sexiest nightie.

In your careful and meticulous work
To erect an edifice of matchless perfection,
You don't see that all erections
Originate from your imperfections.

Proximity

If this majestic mountain of the night
Loses its dark beauty
When I step on its rocky trails by day,
If your beauty is lost when I get too close
And anchor my little boat in your bay,
If the fear to succeed exceeds by far
The fear of failure
And the dreams of yesterday horrify me
More than the reality of today,
If I can smile to my host at dinner,
Sipping his blood for soup
While he serves me the main course
From his flesh on a tray,
If the blind eyes seem to see me in my shame
While the seeing ones shy away,
If growing up requires separation from
My mother's breast and the worm
That fathers me is the one that eats my guts away,
If it's easier to love my homeland from a distance
And sing patriotic songs from far away,
Then you must understand, my beloved,
My friend, my neighbour and my enemy,
That the last person I want to see is me.

THE CITY

Human Resources

No one knows when
Or how it happened.
May be when the children
Stopped loving
Their grandmother.

Or when hashish and marijuana
Became illegal,
While alcohol and cigarettes
Were merely vilified.

Or when men's hands became softer
Holding champagne glasses in
lavish balls
While Children's hands bled stitching
soccer balls.

Or when anorexic young men and women
Posed for the camera
To advertise brands.

Or when wrist watches became
Nicholas Cage's Smile
displayed on the hands,
The briefs Beckham's body
And the bras Victoria's Secret.

Or when traders invented their own
Academic discourses.
No one can tell when human beings
Became human resources.

To A Chinese Poet Whom I Knew

The dried-up well of memory,
The cut wing of imagination,
Only wait menacingly
For yet another disintegration.

O beautiful wanderer and muse,
Come to my thoughts by daylight,
Or if you choose,
Come by night,
Come to me at dawn,
Or indeed at sunset,
With a face that impales the moon.

Let your mouth sing,
Let it promise pleasure,
Let your eyes make a kill,
Feed on my exhausted body.

Poetic inspiration, your presence
In flesh and bones
Only stresses
The impossibility of your presence.

I hold in my hand
A deadly cigarette, a pen, a raging fire.
Victimize my heart,
Inflame my mad desire,
Create my art,
Weaken my limbs,
Turn me to ashes,
But release my ink
With violent lashes.

O Poem, O Christian Mission,
Enter with no permission.
For against what you do
With amazing ease, I think,
Probably,
The wine is trying to irritate me,
The smoke to deaden my feeling.
Both fail
Miserably.

Commuting

When I came to Hong Kong,
People held books and newspapers
In public transportation.
Later they held iPods and music players,
Then smartphones, iPads and tablets.
Nowadays they prefer to sleep
Even through the shortest journey.

Everything is in place – almost catatonic.
What can be done after the technological orgy?
Close your eyes and imagine some past agony;
Life before today's indispensable gadgets
That made daily commuting motionless.
It was difficult, but it was also erotic.
The city was young, inquisitive, horny.
Now I feel old, assured, listless.

The Selfie Stick

It is as if there are dark forces
Bent on isolating every one of us.
The briefest human contact
Is no more commended
And may become downright illegal
Sooner than we think.

Walking down the street with a friend
From the old days fast coming to an end,
We encounter a young man with specs;
The specs looking at a phone screen,
The screen obviously returning the favour,
For the young man seems to be engaged
In a conversation with his rectangular friend.

I stop him and ask him gingerly to click us.
He seems to say "okay", but the "okay"
Doesn't come as it used to on a bygone day.
His squinting eye behind one spec
Seems to pose a legitimate question:
Where is your stick?

Hongkonger

Everyone assumes that I am there,
A Hongkonger;
A businessman, a teacher, a student,
A fishmonger.

They do not realize that in fact I never had a say
In my destiny.
I have always been in between
Powers larger than me.

Yes, I am sheltered, safe, well fed, I mean
I never lacked anything essential.
But I have been invented to make up a city
With an impressive

SKYLINE;
RICH, CONNECTED, COMPACT,
ONLINE.

The politicians keep forgetting though
What makes me deadly lone.
The city exists.
I don't.

Hongkonger in the MTR

I do not pull the edge of my skirt
To cover my knees out of modesty
Or conservatism or public manners,
I do so to deprive men
Of seeing my alabaster skin
And fantasizing about its touch.

And since I wasn't touched that much
In the course of about six years,
I don't care anymore about the little happiness
I get out of the looks.

I am now more concerned about
Ruining their imagination, the notion
Of fantasy maddens me –
The fact that nothing is real anymore.
Men are just too timid, too insecure.

Window shopping is the city's major trait,
But the shopping paradise is a big lie.
Men, nowadays, just like to watch;
They don't go in to buy.

Containers

The history of civilization
Is a history of containment;
Containment of human communities,
Containment of the ravages of nature,
Containment of accumulated knowledge,
Of anger, of frustration.

The brain is a container.
The heart is a container.
The vagina is a container.
What would the world be
Without the notion of containment?

In this exceptionally civilized city,
The container has made history.
After being a container of goods
For so long, anonymously
Stacked with others on liners,
Wharfs, storehouses, and trucks,
It has finally moved up in life,
Broken its chains, escaped definition,
Halted its usual motion, got a promotion.

It became a house, and,
Instead of frozen goodies,
It can now contain bodies.

Ode to a Cheongsam

Who can sleep
When the sun is
Wearing a cheongsam
Unashamedly concisely?

Eyes get tired of
Sleepless nights, and
In moments of great awareness
They weep.
But to maintain their function,
They have to sleep,
Even if briefly.

Yet the eyelids refuse
To be pulled down
And blind the eyesight
In front of a sight
That redefines the use
Of sight.

The sun is wearing
A cheongsam
In an S-shaped form;
Common, yet out of norm,
Oblivious to its surroundings,
Disregarding all the eyes
That get blurred
By its magnificent presence.

The sun occupies a single seat,
Yet seems to unseat
Every other star in the sky.
Who can deny
That the sun is beautiful
Beyond any words?

How can the eyelids let go?
Who doesn't want
To be blinded
Everyday
By looking at the sun
From head to toe?

Completely covered and
At once subtly uncovered
By a cheongsam;
A unique version
That speaks perversion;
A Chinese stab in the back
Which describes thoroughly,
Explores slowly,
Reveals quite painfully,
Unpacks viciously
At each curve and every cove,
Torturing moments
Of unconsummated love.

Brief Encounters I

There is always something
Awkward
When two people meet
In the street.
"Funny hair, but what
Is he looking at?"
"She isn't pretty, but why
Frown on top of that?"
"Gweilo, tall, long-nosed,
Arrogant, complete!"
"Oh, the neighbour, but not
In the neighbourhood.
Better pretend not to notice
As much as possible."
"If she smiles I smile,
If not then not."
"He looks satisfied,
In love, just out of bed.
Let me grin
Even though I wish him dead."
"What a body, what
Beautiful face, and how those
Warm eyes speak, but
I must block my nose."
"He ignores me
Though we never met.
Am I not a woman?"
"She pretends to be
Someone she's not."
"He pretends to be
Something, big shot."
"Poor."
"Rich."
"Asshole."
"Bitch."

Brief Encounters II

There is always something
Awkward
When two people meet
In an elevator;
Strangers in close proximity,
Seeing themselves and each other
In a big mirror.
Eight eyes is just too much to bear
And, above the heads, a ninth –
Big Brother.
They busy themselves by
Looking at the moving numbers over their heads.
Doors open at last.
They fly in terror.

Receptions and Conferences

Reading Dylan's "Deaths and Entrances"
For what could be the hundredth time,
I oddly realize how a good part of my life
Was spent in receptions and conferences;

How I had to converse smilingly with people
About things I can't care less about
Or sit for hours listening to experts
Explaining tables and figures,
Nodding my head from time to time
As if the flow of imports and exports
Were crucial to my life;

Participating enthusiastically in the
Collective stupid grin on the made up faces
Always running for places in capacious spaces
In which those who are supposed to know
Predict the future of the flow
Of money, trade, and investments
To those who sit with troubled intestines
Holding on until the coffee break
Saves them from the grin.

They all look for entrances
To the world of wealth,
Thinking that first they have to go
Through these gates of death.

Amusement

They look intrigued
By the sight of someone
Writing in a little notebook
In a public place.

"What does he have to write?
And write with a pen?!
On paper?"

I think the source of the amusement
Is that they see
Their nostalgia
Right in front of their eyes;
Someone who seems to belong
To the past.

They know it is intentional;
They know
That somewhere in his pockets
There must be something more
Digital,
But they like to imagine something
Fictional;
That there is this man
Who hasn't heard
That people do things differently now.

Old Hongkonger

The hospitals are more crowded than before,
The doctors don't smile anymore,
The queues are getting ever longer,
The walking sticks and weak body parts
From the old city are taken care of
By government programs and charts
Displayed on many screens,
But who can cure the hearts?

Memory is a strange thing.
It intrudes suddenly to put a smile
On the wrinkled faces.

How I wish to go back to my old Hong Kong;
To shut a window that was left ajar,
To feed the sparrow, to listen to the merry voices
Of the neighbours playing mah-jong,
To speak to the children in the playground.
The language is changing;
Getting lighter, loftier, more proper.
It sounds fine, but it isn't mine.

A Hong Kong Artist

In the old tram, she stood beside me in the aisle,
Looking like a cinematic character that
Got out of the screen by accident. She smiled
Cautiously, and that's when it happened,
I thought she had the most adorable smile.

On the first date, she told me about her puppy
And that puppies are more loyal than people
And that she does not like to be touched by men.
"I respect that", I told her, but never called her again.

Seven years later, I met her in the tram for the second time,
She looked older but her smile hasn't changed with time.
On the second date, she told me about her paintings
And that she can discuss anything except sex and men.
"I respect that", I told her, but never called her again.

I kept a picture of her sitting opposite me in a restaurant
Wearing that most adorable smile that trapped me twice
And one of her paintings that she insisted to send me thrice
By email – a pair of absolutely evil eyes
On a featureless, formless, and frameless face
That scared the shit out of me.
What's wrong with this city?!

Ludic Democracy

The children's backs are breaking
Under heavy school bags, but
Hong Kong wants democracy.

Many people live in shared flats,
Lining up in front of toilets, but
Hong Kong wants democracy.

The small shops are disappearing,
Little family businesses cannot survive,
The number of single parents is increasing,
Men and women are losing their sexual drive,
We have more boys and girls with epilepsy,
But Hong Kong wants democracy.

Basic essentials are getting too expensive,
Children often catch their parents pensive,
The rent swallows half of the salary,
But Hong Kong wants democracy.

Fathers and mothers of the middle class,
Overeducated and undervalued by
A market that sees only those who fly
Business class with willing secretaries
Do not know how to argue with their kids
When they tell them that money is everything
In spite of the teachers and the preachers
Of God, of the good, and virtues and modesty,
But Hong Kong wants democracy.

Capitalist Democracy

Papas, patricians, preachers and politicians
Taught us to want her because she's colour blind,
She doesn't see race or categorize a face
Or distinguish between black, white, or pale,
Her mind is one of a kind that doesn't find
Significance, or difference, in any case.

Papas, patricians, preachers and politicians
Taught us to want her because she doesn't choose;
Her standards are market-based fair competitions
In which she neither favours a kind nor spares a find,
In which anyone of any size, shape, age or mind
Can work up, can come on top, none is declined.

Papas, patricians, preachers and politicians
Taught us to want her because she doesn't care
How you pray, to which god, what you profess,
What you do or eat, how you greet or dress,
If you are ugly, or if you stammer, or if you smell,
She accommodates almost everyone, pell-mell.

We want her because she doesn't seem to abhor
Any of us, she's close, she's easy, she's a whore.

Spikes

I'm an exhausted city.
They've been drying me up,
Draining my thalassic drink,
And piercing me with steely spikes,
Imposing on me all kinds
Of competitions.

I have to appear to be
Most extravagant and happy,
Bright, day and night, and carefree
Albeit a city with a certain cement
Individuality.

I have to smile broadly,
Even when they rape me,
Especially when they rape me.

And as they construct me
The only way they were taught to like;
As they shove in me spike after spike,
I construct them back
Stone by stone, I turn them into stone,
I make them lone, frigid and alike.

Advertisements

This
Is a city of advertisements
That you aren't supposed to
Miss;
A dollar sign,
The latest iPhone,
A black muscular 'tiger' in
A Calvin Klein.
You can't choose your rulers
But you can choose how you
Dress.
This
Is a city that makes sure that
You don't go mad
By carrying you forward
From ad to ad;
Everything offers itself
To the onslaught;
The wall, the tunnel,
The station, the train, the
Bus,
The bodies, the buildings,
The brains.
No wonder why
We make sure
To instil in the children
That Toys "R"
Us.

Chinese Café, Hong Kong in 1995

"The menu is in Chinese,
How am I supposed to choose?"
The waitress smiled
And pointed to the dish
In front of my neighbour –
Another confused foreigner
On a single seat table –
And cutely said: "fissssh".
I felt there was no point
Trying to argue with that,
So I said: "okay, fish".
My neighbour smiled knowingly
And told me I was lucky,
At least I knew
What was coming.
Amid the loud voices,
The hearty laughs,
The impenetrable Cantonese,
I realized that one doesn't go
To a local café to eat, but to
Play with the linguistic barrier,
To touch an exotic surface,
To contain oneself inside one's
Foreignness;
To hear more, to see more,
And eat less.

A Hong Kong Winter

Coats in the cold and cats in black;
The shortest season has come back
To the city of concealed cataclysm.
The sharp contrast of skin and cloth,
A glimpse worthy of sculpting studies,
The chafing of touching tails of wool
Doing the job for dead bodies.

Coats in the cold and cats in black,
Carried inside cacophonies,
Buried underneath digital cronies,
Composing a coarse screen to be seen
Casting characters, coursing lives,
Carving curves, holding nerves,
But catching cold is to be avoided at any cost.

Falling in love is what this city sets yet dreads the most.

**The Death of Master Wu Yong Deren, also known as
Mr Yogurt, in the Year 2047**

Wong Lee, we have to write this epitaph carefully
For the sake of future generations.
Master Wu's death was tragic but inevitable,
We've tried everything, but he was intolerable,
Sadly he left us, making his usual empty fuss.

You're our best poet, Wong Lee, you know
What to write about our beloved, Mr Yogurt.
You knew him well, the volatile Wu Yong Deren,
Who desperately wanted to live forever, the one
Who believed he knew how to be in between worlds
And make heaps of money out of the two.

The one who enjoyed himself on both sides of the border,
The rebel who threw himself in the sea without fear
After making sure all the cameras were on
And the rescue team was in full gear.

The one who thought the lap dance a political stance,
The free thinker who didn't know free from what,
The social drinker who exercised every morning
Just to postpone his death and shake his butt
A little more between north, south, east and west.

The pampered Master Wu with the golden spoon
In his mouth since his birth, the born landlord,
The juggernaut of vocal eruptions and illegal structures
Who could afford almost everything at any instance.

The one who always sympathized with those who
Suffered but made sure to do so from a safe distance,
The one with the perfect made up complexion
And glossy mannish muscles, the magnificent Wu,
Who was always conscious of the competition.

The friendly Deren who used to grin broadly,
With his perfect set of white teeth in our parties,
While someone else fucked his wife upstairs.

Compose your phrases with great care, Wong Lee!
We want everyone to know we didn't kill him ourselves,
He died of happy flatulence in a perfect democracy.

The City of Screens

Without ever meeting,
We're already heartbroken,
On many screens;
Digital love speeding
Everyone to the point
Of total disappearance
Before the body has its way.

How do we maintain
What's perpetually maintained
In a radical way?
How can we enjoy
When enjoyment is a mandate,
An unpretentious button
Urging a simple update?

How can we appear
When our bodies are ever present,
Saturated with scents and senses,
Sensitive to the digit,
Yet of them we have no awareness?
And though I long for touching
The belly of a dancing Dionysus,
I know that the deity, in this city,
Has been frozen, broken to little pieces
And spread over millions of screens.

Beloved stranger appearing
As running text to me,
Do not imagine I have access
To any written decree,
I can only feel the excess
Of what you write as sealed
Christmas gifts on a tree
With a thousand little lights,

Even if you don't intend it to be.

To write is to be born, to live and to die.
To read is to save, to waste, to cry.
The letters are clear, WE are overstated
On those screens.

Just as a mirage we've always been,
Illusory visions, never genuine,
A handful of seawater, evaporated,
And bitter salt remained to tell
Of those volatile, running,
Crystal blue drops,
Rapidly vanishing in a scroll
That never stops.

The Forbidden City

The forbidden city
Is not to the north,
It's right here in our hearts,
We see it everyday with
No access to its rich parts.

It takes as much as
Walking in the street
To greet its imposing presence,
The eye cannot mistake
Its purpose, the mind frets
When it fast fathoms its essence.

Our forbidden city
Is forbidden as a modern
Glass and steel work of kitsch art
To behold, a feast for the eyes.

Our forbidden city
Has a formidable foundation,
Boasting the fiction of self-creation.

Our forbidden city
Is also forbidding;
Built out of a stock market
Where the universe is prostituted,
It forbids most social relations.

Our forbidden city
Is also foreboding;
Below the shiny surface
There is raw anger, there is fire,
Behind the beautiful face
A deadly dagger.

Beyond the dull domestication
A spirit longing to be freer.

Numbered

I am a person of great integrity,
Like my father,
By the time I walked and my society
Let me enter,
Admitting me in its long register
As dad's junior,
I was taught to respect the elderly,
As well as bow to His Majesty
The Grand Number.

And when the number of candles
In my thick birthday cake lost
Significance,
I realized that everything in
This existence
Has a number as its cost,
Even people, indeed people in
Particular.

Nothing escapes the Majestic Number;
The god that doesn't drowse or slumber
All year long, in the spring, summer
Fall or winter,
And subordinates everything else,
Inseminating the universe,
Reproducing endlessly its
Monstrous creature.

I was trained in the sense of the old god
Of money, and told that life remains good
As long as most numbers go up
No matter what and the rich
Are made richer.

Born in a shed, born in a palace or a
Secret bunker,
I was born enclosed in numbers,
And taught I should out of them
Make an armour.
I live numbers, I eat numbers,
I drink numbers, and I will surely
Croak for numbers.

I was told that when I die my family
Members will have to remember,
Before they cry,
My grave number,
Not just for mourning; more for keeping
On an altar
The ultimate worship for my posterity,
The sign of my numerical integrity.

I Dreamt of a Mask

I dreamt of a mask
Enshrined as saviour
Of a city felled anew
Several times over.

A white mask turned green,
A green one turned blue,
Before the black mask
Made an entrance
As a matter of taste,
Trending itself and
Creating turnover
Through pale K-pop idols
Fast filling every kiosk,
Insinuating through the mist,
In states of sickness and health,
Each and every face and flesk,
Making it easy, with no smile, to misk
And mistake the kiss for a serious risk.

I dreamt of a mask
Holding sway over a city,
Putting it to the test,
Like a god hungry for sacrifice
Of the bent bone and the newborn
That cannot satisfy or suffice,
Grinding them all down to the marrow,
Waving the deadly shadow of the past
To shun, to run to see tomorrow
And bask in the light of the last sun.

The runners developed a sickly fitness
That made history's plagues pale,
And though they were so tempted to die mask-less,
Their own hands made sure to fail

That last desire of the confined heart.
The blackout was sudden and death was fast.

Heather

Welcome to our great theatre!
Where day and night you can meet Heather,
The city's best invention ever!

The nymph cannot get any better,
And thou shalt see her everywhere,
In her neat outfit, hybrid and hyper,
Carrying her hypnotized hard head
And angular hips with a shimmer.

On the day of her blithe baptism,
We made sure to sculpt her
Hot beauty and the firm body,
But eliminate her orgasm.

And with pallid passion she shall greet you
With her perfect cinematic mouthpart,
Drawn by a mechanical hollow heart,
Manufactured under our hands.

Mark the valid fashion! Buy one get two!
Looking foxy and aptly slimmer;
We don't tire of tweaking Heather.

Musical as the nightingale is her voice,
Pure and oblivious to the notion of vice,
She flowers fast in any weather,
And spreads like a good heavenly song.

However, you shouldn't get that wrong;
Heather is a daughter, a sister, a lover,
And, if intent, can be one hell of a mother!

She's the ultimate dream come true of man,
She can talk, walk, make love and compete,

Though frigid, she parades hidden heat,
The ungotten ghost of a gaunt woman,
Heather is our city's greatest treasure.

She toils tirelessly and gives us pleasure
With her cellophane surface of artificial
Skin and the sly hypocritical smile,
Even her hypocrisy is superficial.

Therefore, ultimately true to us and herself
Much more than we can ever be to one another.
At desks, homes, on the road, or kept on a side shelf,
Her presence, in a sense, keeps us checked, but, together.

And, finally, our beloved customer,
Please pay attention to what is written
With almost invisible letters on the cover:
'Handle with care! Perishable but lives forever!'

A Fulfilled Promise

Absolutely diabolical in her savage charm,
The city smiled and seemed to promise him reinvention.
He was afraid to fail, so he failed to fall in her arms,
And decidedly determined to be undetermined,
Feeling fellows following firm and crystal convictions
Come off colonial deformities malformed entities,
Knowingly recognizing the stiff fragile foundation
Upon which awkwardly penetrated ancient nations
Try to come to terms with the flimsy new identities
Born of fear and fire and frowned upon fornication.

But the image of happy love birds burnt his heavy heart
And fed on the flimsy film of the framed sulking spirit,
The odd timidity within the fragmented body
That failed and yet filled those pages with crafty sullen art.

And thus the city somehow fulfilled her age-old promise;
The furry fiend of love frightened his non-flying wings, cut
And kept always checked, shackled within tired yet raised
arms,
The fire of desire ferociously filled his psalms,
The sign of full-fledged failure, the devil's stabbing kiss.
And finally, they laid him half-dead upon his death bed,
With a sea of fiery words jumbling his big white head.
The city winked at her mess, mocking his eternal loss.

WOMAN

Plain Woman

Beware the unremarkable female,
The type no one looks at twice,
The type with listless features
And common demeanour,
With one hand holding
On to something, the other hanging
Mid-air in front of her
As if she is clueless about
What to do with it.

The one whose smile
Does not say anything,
The one whose body
Looks like a flat landscape,
The one whose eyes
Neither tell the truth nor lie,
The one who neither attracts
Nor repels anyone.

The one who has no fragrance
Of her own, and does not leave
Any traces when she passes by,
The one whom you do not notice
Even when no other is around,
The invisible one who walks in
And no one raises their head.

For this is the one
Whose love will end your life;
This is the one whose passion in bed
Will leave you disoriented in disbelief;
This is the one whose volatility
Will drive you to madness.

This the one
Who's better than none,
Equal to none,
Possessing no weapon.
Beware the plain woman!

Sign

Unless you show up as my personal moon
And wink playfully through the light,

Unless you submit your being entirely
To my whimsical thoughts and night-
Bound biting bits of little cruelties,

Unless you tremble in my arms and eyes
Like a dry leaf in a windy day,

Unless you crucify yourself for me
And let me hear the sound of your agony,

Unless you transform yourself into a sign
Of my mighty munching mechanic manhood
And act as if you are completely mine,

I can never be a man without your pantomime.

You may have been created to make me erect,
But I am destined to be your side-effect.

Mother

The dark realm always calls
Its own never to return;
Never to go back or look back.

It knows its incredible power;
It knows that its great love
In spite of everything can devour,
Can destroy a whole life or burn
Every relation before it takes shape.

For nothing stands in between man
And his mysterious sealed puddle
But that flimsy film of floating
Images devised to conceal the elapse
Of time and hardly prevent the collapse
Of this recreant before he suffers
The whole way from womb to tomb.

Anxiety

Anxiety
In front of your photograph
Is neither simply a sign of love
Nor a pervert's imagination.
It is more on the side of
Piety,
A text dismantled by an epitaph,
Achilles killed by a little arrow
Through his heel.
This is not just adoration,
But ultimately my fragmentation.

She

Unable to reach an intellectual compromise,
She challenged me to a long stare;
The one who blinks first fails.

I didn't know what I was getting into
When the game started to take a serious turn;
The stand assumed a position of a fight to death,
And while I was mainly distracted
By the proximity of her beautiful face,
She was more focused on winning the contest.

I am not a quitter though,
And I was determined to do my best.

Eyeing the defiance in my eyes,
She seemed to summon a new energy
From somewhere within her delicate frame.
The dark eyes looked me straight in the face.
I gathered all my strength in order not to flinch,
When all of a sudden I felt I wasn't just facing
A woman I knew, but a force of nature –
A silence louder than any sound,
A darkness brighter than any light.

I've always claimed to have a finer sense
And a better awareness of the big questions,
But then she seemed to have possession
Of smaller and bigger things of a different nature,
As if beyond our location inside the little room
In one of those closed cement structures of the city,
Distant voices came to her ears
From the jungles of the world.

Millions of little feet advanced towards her body;
Little creatures of every sort and shape crawled
Up the walls to come to her assistance,
And deep inside and all around me
I could feel a subtle mobility in existence.

All the blind worms of the earth were with her.
The fallen tree leaves of the fall flew in upon her call.
The frenzied flies of every dungy corner
Came in buzzing in my ear.

The dust particles, the microbes, the viruses,
The airborne diseases were with her.
The blood within my own body was on her side.
It took some time before I realized
That I've been blinking wildly,
And when she got enough, she finally smiled
And said with the good old humility:
"See? I told you I was right".

Distraction

I am distracted by woman;
Losing my bearings completely
At the slightest gesture.
Her presence cancels thought,
Impedes writing,
Produces naught.
She renders literature a lie,
Culture just a joke,
Civilization something born
To die.
Nothing survives nature
Or disciplines desire.
She knows she is a fire
In the vicinity of thin paper,
A deadly digger of a ditch of death
Where love oddly appears
And man disappears.

Inspiration

Every piece of writing tries
To put a woman on paper,
Every poem is cut out
Of bits and pieces of her body,
Every letter is addressed to her,
Every drop of ink and blood
Comes out of her, returns to her.

To write is to recognize
The world in her figure,
To write is to see God
Through the miracle of her presence,
To write is to submit oneself
To her, even if she isn't there.

All that is written,
In essence, in true sense,
Is written by a woman,
Written because of a woman,
Written for a woman.
And what keeps this going on,
What keeps writers forever smitten
On pages of burning pyre
Is that she remains ever unwritten.

The Unattainable One

No one stays long in the place
Of the unattainable one.
The illusion can be created
For the slightest reasons;
It can be a strand of hair
On the forehead,
Or the shape of a nose,
Or a certain set of teeth,
Or prominent cheekbones.

What causes the fall, every time,
Promises the unattainable one,
That which is not even defined,
A fragrance nobody breathed yet,
Music unheard of,
Curvy landscapes never captured
In imaginations,
Orifices giving entirely
New sensations,
Impossible features and gestures
That escape common experience.

Vision can be distorted by desire
To allow a glimpse
At the impossible one
Through an object of love.
It makes enjoyment a possible lot,
Every time,
Of a woman who is here
Through a woman who is not.

Flowers

Flowers don't understand,
They don't compromise,
They either inhale
All the breezes of spring
Or die,
Integrity is their stand.
The lover's prize
Makes him pale,
The kiss is itself a sting,
A goodbye.

In their beauty and tenderness,
Lies their very mercilessness,
Vase fillers, soft killers,
They never transgress
Any boundaries.
They stay still
Until
Lovers fail to guess
The time of disappearance
And eternal loss.

Flowers just
Don't understand
What they do
Offhand.

Believer

Behind the veil and the fear
She knows that she threatens
The fall of God into sin.

As a true believer she adheres
Literally to the Word
And the Word belongs to Him.

She, however, has no say
In it, and loves it that way.

For once it speaks, the divine
Enters into a binding contract
That makes it less sublime,
Negotiable, representable, a fact
Like any other, a linguistic product.

Talking to God is not simply prayer;
She knows that the dialogue
Captures Him in the snare of desire –
A desire to own the body of the believer,
To enter it, to fill it, to tire
Its organs, to torture it to death.

Behind the veil and the fear,
The trembling and the panting breath,
She knows that she is a pit
In which God and His lesser men
Fall every day but hate to admit
That her exclusion from their
Symbolic universe destroys it.

The Other Woman

The other woman is supposed to come
From another world, and to carry within
Babylon the Great.

She should create the illusion of a promise
Of something more than a void between her legs.

She should have a face that smiles,
Cries, demands, and begs all at once.

She should do all that is right for all that is wrong –
Vicious like a Juliette with the heart of a Suzie Wong.

She should conceal herself from the lusting eyes
Of men, but let me exercise mine on her
And exorcise her demons, one by one,
Like a Jesus healing a Mary Magdalene.

The other woman should be a powerful Theodora,
Demanding, commanding, unashamed of her past
Or her body's flourishing fauna and flora,
Reigning in the wind, the wilderness, the world.

She should be larger than life, her taste
Should be the taste of full-bodied wine,
The type that finds its way easily fast and deep,
Edging desire, sapping the body, disturbing sleep.

The other woman should be a Rahab, a Mata Hari,
Prizing secrecy and stealth in love as the greatest wealth.

She should know about the undeclared bond
Between the speaking law and the dark unspoken,
She should know that laws are made by men
And their gods primarily in order to be broken.

She should know that the peaceful smile of the priest
Preaches God and hides the devil's grin within,
And that the gods made life an odd mix of milk
And meat and laughs and cries and wine and gin.

The other woman should be a Phryne and an Aspasia;
You shouldn't be able to tell whether she comes
From the lands of Europe or Africa or Asia.

She should be as ancient as Egypt, with endless
Chinese masks and unknowable Indian spices.

She should know how to seduce without seducing
And produce without producing consuming passion,
Seductive fragrances and intense sexual fury.

She should know when and how to reveal her breasts
In the court of law and astound the judge and jury.

She should know what to say on Judgement Day –
God created life, and she lived it, her way.

Hymen

The list of poets who contemplated hymen
Is an endless one.
Perhaps its invisibility adds to its enigma.
Perhaps its eventual entire disappearance
Casts a shadow on its liminal existence.

Hymen is the name of something ripped
By an inquisitive look and an assenting nod,
But it is also the name of a Greek god,
The son of a muse who took delight in dancing.
It cannot be dissociated from 'hymn';
Human imagination seems to assume something
So subtle, so weak, so strong, so hard to define
Must be of a different order, must be divine.

Yet unlike ancient gods, hymen doesn't appear,
Unlike God, it doesn't commend or condemn,
In its hideout and absolute silence, it stays
Too 'hy', a secret prayer without an 'Amen',
In its sometimes unbelievable elasticity,
It gestures a defiant 'hy!' to 'men'.

My first encounter with hymen
Was an unforgettable one;
It was more ceremonial than anything else,
As if the event was to be registered
By me, by her, by the angels and the demons
Who must have witnessed hymen's demise.

There was melancholy in the spilled blood,
And because culture makes the bloody business
Almost a divine order,
It does feel like a killing, a murder.

I found no enjoyment in hymen's encounter,

And, that which came later in the name
Of pleasure always carried a sad reminder;
Nothing came to bloom without post-coitus gloom.

Aria

The feminine aria in an opera
Reveals with no doubt
That at its core, the song
Of woman isn't supposed
To have a meaning,
Isn't supposed to communicate
Something intelligible.

It is her being
Delivered in a scream,
Humanity's worst dream
To be entirely dominated
By the primitive,
To be traumatized
By uncontrolled nature,
To be reminded
Of the tyranny of voice,
To lose religion,
And literature,
To lose our bearings
Without a text,
To be torn from reality
And context,
To be exposed to unmediated
Knowledge,
To skip the outer skin and touch
The blood,
To bypass mediators and face
God.

The aria is a fracture
In the universe,
A distortion, a collapse,
A curse.
The aria is human,

But also inhuman.
The aria is
Woman.

Mark

She looked at herself in the mirror
Admiring the mark my teeth impressed
On her nebulous white skin and said,
"It was painful, but how glorious it looks now."

A strange silence followed.

Did we enjoy the brief moment
Of inflicting pain and taking it?
Or did we do it in expectation
Of seeing the mark appear
As evidence that something
Did happen and we call it love?

As if love which didn't show itself
On the body wasn't enough;
We had to leave a trace to prove
That we lived, loved, gave ourselves.

It had to be recorded in some register.
It had to be somehow written somewhere.
From birth to maturity, the mark is a poem
Carved out with passion, published posthumously.

The Goddess of Chaos Talks to Equus

You should mind my new status,
Equus.
I am now a married woman.

You shouldn't stare at me like that
With those big eyes of yours.

You shouldn't sniff at my hair
And my neck the way you do
Anymore.

Above all,
You shouldn't be excited
When you see me.
This is totally embarrassing.

You cannot expect
Anyone of them to understand.
They are natural-born liars,
And they know it, even though
They tell themselves, day and night,
That "they know not what they do".

Equus,
We have no choice but to go
Our separate ways, you,
On four, and I, unfortunately,
On two
But, I will never forget you.

ALTERNATIVE HISTORIES

Henry VIII in His Stables on the 28th of January 1547

Canicida, let me caress your neck,
Run my hand over your side,
Touch your mane, smell your hide.

You were her closest friend, her confidant,
Sometimes I think she loved you more
Than she loved me, fed you with her
Own hands, graced you with her light being,
Gave you pleasure by the warmth of her thighs,
Bent over to whisper in your ear
So that your neck could feel her heavenly breasts,
And, every time, dismounted and faced you
So that you can smell her hair and cheeks.

You have seen my envious eyes burning you
Without mercy. Many a time I thought about
Killing you out of jealousy.

My innocent queen, fairer than daylight,
Loved by me, by all men, by her maids,
By the horses, by the flowers in the garden,
The stones of the palace, the stars, the night.

By the swordsman who took her life.

Her neck, Canicida! Her neck! O hell, take us all!
I declare her innocence in front of you,
Noble friend, uncorrupted by religion,
And ask you to pray for my soul.

Two Egyptian Lovers, Tel-el-Amarna In 1327 B.C.

Huya, look at what I found!
This bust belongs to the late queen
THE BEAUTIFUL ONE HAS COME.
The soldiers must have missed it
When they tore everything down.

Behold the long neck, the delicate face
Of our dear mother, Lady of Grace.
They say she used to lie naked under the sun.
Her husband, the late king, was a saint
Who talked like a woman, and walked like one,
Yet, of power and dominance he stripped Amun
And gave them to our only god,
The magnificent Atun.

But it was she, our Lady of all Women
Who taught us to expose our bodies to Him,
To get cleansed while we bask in his light.
Huya, make love to me! Consecrate the night!
This time not by the order of our hearts,
But by that of the Lady of the Two Lands.
Let us honour her appearance to our humble selves
In this country which no longer understands
That deities emanate from our bodies
And return to them.

***

They knew nothing of far darker ages to come;
Of covered bodies and coerced heads
That shy away from the sun;
Of nightmares about women hung by the nipples;
Of gloved hands and concealed faces;
Of the body as chief enemy of the people,
As an animal made to appear timidly in closed cages.

The bust however was lucky, and the queen,
Eventually, was safely smuggled to Berlin.
Germany, I beg you, don't listen to anyone!
Never return the queen of the sun!

Potiphar's Wife Visiting Joseph in Jail

Can you deny that you loved
Me as much as I loved you?
Can you deny you shivered
Every time my hand touched
Your hand, that you trembled
Every time you poured my wine?

That you blushed when you bent
Over too much to smell my scent
And kept gazing at my sipping lips?
That you pretended to pick up dregs
From the floor to get the briefest glimpse
Of what is between my legs?

That you masturbated more than once
In your hiding place watching me undress
And made love to me in your dreams?
That you shook violently at night,
Moaning, calling me filthy names?

If you can deny all that, you are a fraud,
A false prophet. If you can't, make love
To me! Take me! Make me believe in your God!

A Group of Christian Monks, Alexandria in 415 A.D.

Let all speculate as they wish,
But she, barely dressed, confessed
Her own deviations from the truth.

We do condemn her corrupt mind,
Her deplorable pagan thoughts,
But the real problem is, her youth.

This body which speaks its own pleasure!
This body which does not take fright!
Those eyes darker than the night!

The two half-naked breasts! The maddening hair!
The tongue that reaches out in passion, in honesty,
Far more dangerous than that which speaks philosophy.

This body has to be mutilated, gored.
The wench is more beautiful than our Lord!
What else calls for a greater punishment?

More beautiful than Him?!
That imperfect creature with too many orifices?!
With this darkness between her legs?!
The deadly trench, the unpredictable blood, the stench?!

She's a freak, who does not only speak – she enjoys.
Her philosophy, the world, the Lord are but her toys.
One can almost see her twisting, hear her sinful moans.
Collect the stones!! Collect the stones!!

Aufidius After the Death of Martius

"Let me twine mine arms about that body",[i]
The supreme object of my wars and my love.

Let us lie necking for the last time.
O the smell of the skin, the taste of your blood!

What will remain of Aufidius, what life
Can be lived without the strife,
The foe who is dearer than my wife?

The face that is getting cold,
that I scoffed and kissed I know not how many times,
Is what made me recognize the world
For what it is; a show veiling a story untold
Of love residing at the very heart of enmity,
And desire in the very body we hurt the most,
Injuring ourselves with our own weaponry.

In mourning shall I remain for the rest of my life,
Conjuring your image in battles and in bed.
The numbness I feel in my body will drive
My hand to the kill with no heart, and in my head
The memory of Martius will rule unequalled,
With each mark on my body blessing his sword
That made me a warrior of love and hate,
And left me a widower, living and yet, dead.

The Shrewdness of Odysseus

Met by absolute silence at the island of the sirens,
The sailors started to panic:
"If they don't sing, and if we don't block our ears,
What will become of us without our fears?"

They turned to Odysseus for advice.
"Captain, there is no singing, no nebulous bodies,
No winking eyes, no danger, no vice,
The island looks deserted, the sea is calm,
Its waves are not hitting the rocks as you said,
And the rocks do not look like women's thighs.

The ship is not pulled by any force, and the dead
Sailors' skeletons are nowhere to be seen
On the shore. Against what shall we direct our cries?
From what dark abyss, from what hellish hole
Are we going to escape? Indeed, who have we been
Before coming here, if here denies us all?"

The shrewd Odysseus waved his hand and closed his eyes.
He kept still for a while, then all of a sudden
Trembled as they wouldn't understand the idea of
trembling,
And like a holy man started mumbling
Words that were immediately written;
Words with a meaning that will remain forever 'hidden',
Laying a 'divine law', forbidding and forbidden.

His eyes opened, pierced his men's bodies like stingers,
His ears bled as he stabbed them with his own fingers,
Then he screamed: "the sirens are singing!
Block your ears! Tie me to the mast!"

The sailors still couldn't hear anything,
But his assertion as commander-in-chief,
As leader, as prophet, as both crew and cast,
Made them distrust their sanity and their senses.

"The sirens are singing!" they shouted at each other,
"Get the ropes! Get the wax! All of our defences!
Tie Odysseus! As he loves the sirens like no other!"
So wildly they rowed with all their strength
To save themselves from the island of death.

***

Tied to the mast with wax in his bleeding ears,
Odysseus, stark naked, embraced the wood and wept.
Gone are the fears, the land of no identity.
It feels good to be sane, to shed a few tears.
It feels even better to define insanity.

Dr Rank's Final Words to Torvald

Dearest friend, I cannot receive death
Before unburdening my heart
Which always resided in your house,
Waiting for the slightest touch, the briefest
Kiss, the chafing of the dress, O Torvald,
I am both glad and sad to confess
That for many years what kept me alive
Was the fierce desire to fuck your wife.

Abraham's Wife

What?! Slaughter my son?!
To hell with you and your god!
For what good have you both
Concocted this bloody deal?
For testing your blind loyalty,
Your obedience, your faith, your fear,
Your ridiculous sense of duty?
And where am I in this divine plot?
Am I supposed to stay silent
And just watch the superman order
The old man murder the young man
In this man-to-man grand plan?
Well I don't care about your mad dream,
Incantations, big picture, cosmic scheme,
I don't care about your revelations,
Or miracles, or what you said He said.
Lay a finger on my son and you're dead.

***

And it came to pass that God saved
The promising young man
With a ram.
No, He saved his mighty prophet
From this inhuman
Business –
This betrayal of the self.
No, He saved
Himself.
Abraham's wife smiled in relief.
She never mentioned her role in this.
She chose to keep up appearances.

Baal Coming to Thebes

The flow of our river seems to be gay,
The sweet dry breeze blessing the day.
The drunken tree swaying for the bird,
The singing bird returning the favour,
Spreading its wings, while its heart beat
Rises, the branch coy from its delicate feet.

Mothers abandoning being on their guard,
The children enjoying playing with the mud,
Making miniatures of the visiting god.
In jubilation, our whole nation turns bard.
Tired we are from our lives' monotony,
Its stability, its safety, those bodies that
"Fall back to the walls, into Egyptian darkness".[ii]
Baal is coming to give us new forms of art,
Of lovemaking, of madness; to change our
Unchanging desires and renew our blood.

***

The priests gather in the temple of Ptah,
Perceiving seeds of a dangerous revolt,
Helped by 'foreign elements' from the Levant,
Against Pharaoh himself and against Ra.

They flock to the palace in countless numbers
And on their way plead in panic:
"Good Thebans, come back to your senses,
Baal is wild, lustful, manic.

He will turn you into pigs and ruin your lives,
Enter your houses uninvited and seduce your wives,
And your men, eat up your harvest, drink your wine,
Abuse your children, and do it with the cattle.
Our river will be turned into a dump for dead women.

Savage Charm   117

This is no battle, no test of our soldiers' mettle,
This is a takeover of our Theban way of life,
A destruction of our traditions – the castle
Which protects us from the outside world!"

***

Great Pharaoh, Thebes is in danger
And your seat of power is threatened;
Among our people, Levantines have spies,
Worshippers of Baal, the god of chaos,
With all the dung, the stench, the flies,
The drunken heads and the sick hearts
Locked forever in the lower body parts.
Powerful son of Ra, give your orders,
Send the army to protect the borders.

***

He came to Thebes but never resided there,
The god kept eyeing her from far away,
Always run-down by the journey through Sinai,
Worried about getting killed by the scorching sun.
But, above all, turning into a picture on the wall
Made him pale – he preferred to be a Theban tale.

Horatio after Hamlet's Death

Driven to madness and death by a ghost,
He has made a ghost out of me.
My "sweet prince",[iii] gone, Horatio undone.
Horatio;
The very name seems to refer to no one,
A living dead, on a secret bed
Which still carries his weight, not mine.
"Horatio", uttered by him, his voice
Echoed, shattered, battered my being,
My eyes still seeing
His hands, shoulders, lips and sword,
The cutting sword, the cutting word, the sharp wit.
The problem is, my prince, there is no story to tell,
I only have images and visions,
I only have a body which I don't feel, it fell
Into an abyss, weightless, lifeless.
Better be in the "undiscovered country"
Than lie down here and to myself confess
Melancholy over your lost body.
Horatio undone. Horatio. History.

Bertha Talking to Herself in the Attic

Bertha, I told you countless times to be quiet.
I told you not to cross the master of the house.
You can't expect that visitor of the night
To come when you are so loud.

You're embarrassing him and his whole universe,
You're giving them reason your mind isn't right.
The housekeepers must be winking, secretly giggling.
This is not ladylike, this is not English ethics.

Read your Bible, Shakespeare, logic, physics.
You can't dance, Bertha, you must be proper,
Specially that you have those curvy extras which,
Well, do not sit well with this country of the upright,
The uptight, the stiff upper lip, the lipped apartheid.

And why were you playing with your cutlery
And with your food on the dinner table?
Why were you talking so merrily with the butler,
The valet, the cook, the gardener, the common people?
You've ruined it all, Bertha, nothing now but misery.

✳✳✳

Master, speaker, sneaker, spanker, fucker, thanker!
Drinker, shrinker, madder, swearer, floppy anchor!
Bertha, shady lady, little princess from the island
Where the sun sets at the outskirts of the Empire!
The southern climate, the dark sphere, the exotic fire!
The butt of the world, to be tried, with responsibility!
Bertha! Supposed to tremble in front of her discoverer!
Bertha! Supposed to conform to the best of her ability!
The talking doll! The singing doll! The swinging doll!
The screaming doll who should suppress her scream!
The dreamer who's not supposed to dream!

Dolls do have orgasms, you know?!
The master of the house couldn't take it!
It jumbled words coming out of his mouth!
The dark inexplicable force of the south!
The mystic intervention of someone else!
Of a god who cannot be in any Bible!
Who cannot be anywhere in your writings!
My own god! My own lover! My own universe!
That which cannot be sung by your mannered verse!
The night visitor snapped when he knew I understand
His deficiencies, that I don't really care that much
Because my god comes out of my own hand,
Unfailing, sedulous and so remote from such
Master, speaker, sneaker, spanker, fucker, thanker,
Drinker, shrinker, madder, swearer, floppy anchor!

***

It comes as no surprise after all that has been said,
Bertha's voice is a problem, in literature and in bed.

Poe, Baltimore on the 3rd of October 1849

This city of aliens concealing the solitude of everyone
living
In it walking the streets feeling the coldness of being
In a festive gregarious crowd looking at itself without
seeing
Its gloomy face and the narrow space given to those
unwilling
To pace with maintaining the façade or playing the
masquerade
Now looks at me in my borrowed attire covering the
borrowed
Body containing the alien soul unhearing the rapping
Of the "beak" in my heart eager to put me to sleep forever
unaware
That I myself decided to exit its theatre and leave behind
my art
To those speculating about the lonely poet hallucinating
In the streets of Baltimore but alas this rhyme will be read
"nevermore"[iv]

Burying Ishmael

Earth to earth, ashes to ashes, dust to dust,
Let's sincerely pray and pour the libations
Carefully on the grave of Ishmael,
The last one from the perished nations.

We never really understood him, but,
We do wish him well and hope that
He finally made it to his imagined lush
Garden of all possible gratifications,
After living all of his miserable life
In self-imposed shackles within shreds
And white sheets within shanties and sheds,
Chained, shot, shredded and charred
In those crammed concentration camps
Reducing that excess of flesh to the mush
He deplored, cheered, and cherished
At once, clean and filthy at once, humble
And arrogant at once, a unique pacifist
Warmonger, symbol of gluttony and hunger
At once, dashing smashing religious fascist,
Who was as sinful and guilty as any of us,
But alas, not smart or shrewd enough to push
Himself to fathom that he lived in denial and
Never had the brains for one instance to admit
Without prejudice he was a full bucket of bullshit.

Poor Ishmael, the proud sheep shearer who
Was always already sheared by his preachers –
Those who shaped his past, present and future –
Died drowning in his own thick blood,
With the same ideas in his head like a mesh
Thriving with the maggots of his own ideal shit,
Yet smiling quite broadly, assured of his prospect,
Fortified by what he thought was carte blanche
To Eden, to women, to the divine free lunch.

Poor Ishmael and his endless incantations,
Which blurred his eyes and his mind at once
To the fact he was a nuisance we had to hush.

Bibliography

Adorno, Theodor W. *The Authoritarian Personality*. Edited by Max Horkheimer and Samuel H. Flowerman. NY: Norton, 1969.

Brecht, Bertolt. *Three Plays: Baal, A Man's A Man, The Elephant Calf*. Edited by Eric Bentley. New York: Grove Press, 1964.

Derrida, Jacques. *The Gift of Death*. Translated by David Wills. Chicago & London: The University of Chicago Press, 1995.

Forster, E. M. *Alexandria: A History and a Guide*. London: Michael Haag LTD, 1982.

Freud, Sigmund. *Art and Literature*. Edited by Albert Dickson. Translated from the German under the general editorship of James Strachey. Penguin Books, 1990.

Lacan, Jacques. *The Four Fundamental Concepts of Psycho-Analysis*. Edited by Jacques Alain Miller and translated by Alan Sheridan. Penguin Books, 1994.

Lacan, Jacques. *The Ethics of Psychoanalysis 1959–1960*. Edited by Jacques-Alain Miller and translated by Dennis Porter. London: Routledge, 1999.

Lacan, Jacques. *Écrit: The First Complete Edition in English*. Translated by Bruce Fink. New York and London: W.W. Norton and Company, 2006.

Lévinas, Emmanuel. *Collected Philosophical Papers*. Translated by Alphonso Lingis. Dordrecht, the Netherlands: Nijhoff, 1987.

Nietzsche, Friedrich. *The Gay Science.* Edited by Bernard Williams. Translated by Josefine Nauchhoff. Cambridge, NY, Melbourne: Cambridge University Press, 2001.

Nietzsche, Friedrich. *Thus Spoke Zarathustra.* Edited by Bill Chapko. Based on the Thomas Common Translation. Feedbooks, 2010. Retrieved June 5, 2018, from https://nationalvanguard.org/books/Thus-Spoke-Zarathustra-by-F.-Nietzsche.pdf.

Poe, Edgar Allan. *Great Tales and Poems.* New York: Vintage Books, a division of Random House, Inc., 2009.

Shakespeare, William. *Three Roman Plays: Julius Caesar, Antony and Cleopatra, Coriolanus.* Edited by Norman Sanders, Emrys Jones and G. R. Hibbard. London & New York: Penguin Books, 1994.

Shakespeare, William. *Hamlet.* Edited by G. R. Hibbard. United Kingdom: Oxford University Press, 1998.

The Bible: Authorized King James Version with Apocrypha. Oxford and New York: Oxford University Press, 1998.

Walker, Barbara G. *Man Made God: A Collection of Essays.* Seattle, WA: Stellar House Publishing, LLC, 2010.

Žižek, Slavoj. *Interrogating the Real.* Edited by Rex Butler and Scott Stephens. London and New York: Continuum, 2006.

Žižek, Slavoj. *The Žižek Reader.* Edited by Elizabeth Wright and Edmond Wright. Oxford and Malden, MA: Blackwell Publishing, 1999.

Žižek, Slavoj. *Did Somebody Say Totalitarianism? Five Interventions in the (Mis)use of a Notion*. London and New York: Verso, 2002.

Filmography

The Prince of Egypt. Directed by Brenda Chapman, Simon Wells and Steve Hickner. Written by Philip LaZebnik and Nicholas Meyer. United States: DreamWorks, 1998.

Advance Comments

"In his poetic debut, *Savage Charm*, Elbeshlawy takes us on an exotic trajectory into his own idiosyncratic world. This collection is a collage of the personal intertwined with the impersonal, reality with fantasy and philosophy with eroticism. Almost every poem has something intriguing that provokes the reader's thoughts and mindsets."

—Sayed Gouda, PhD, Poet, novelist, translator, editor.

"Ahmed Elbeshlawy's work is at its most interesting when he concentrates his acute mental lens on his immediate Hong Kong surroundings More, for all of his erudite references to Žižek and Lacan, this poet is essentially a Romantic; his idiosyncratic tropes and topoi entrenched deep in this tradition. "Savage Charm", then, is especially apposite as a title for this collection.."

—Vaughan Rapatahana, PhD, Poet, literary critic, essayist and novelist, winner of the inaugural Proverse Poetry Prize.

Notes

ⁱ Shakespeare, William. *Three Roman Plays: Julius Caesar, Antony and Cleopatra, Coriolanus*. Edited by Norman Sanders, Emrys Jones and G. R. Hibbard. London & New York: Penguin Books, 1994. p. 606.

ⁱⁱ Brecht, Bertolt. *Three Plays: Baal, A Man's A Man, The Elephant Calf*. Edited by Eric Bentley. New York: Grove Press, 1964. p. 42.

ⁱⁱⁱ Shakespeare, William. *Hamlet*. Edited by G. R. Hibbard. United Kingdom: Oxford University Press, 1998. p. 352.

^{iv} Poe, Edgar Allan. *Great Tales and Poems*. New York: Vintage Books, a division of Random House, Inc., 2009. pp. 22-23.

POETRY PUBLISHED BY PROVERSE HONG KONG IN ENGLISH

Alphabet by Andrew Simpson Guthrie

Astra and Sebastian by L.W. Illsley (*teenage epic*)

The Bliss of Bewilderment by Birgit Bunzel Linder

The Burning Lake by Jonathan Locke Hart

Celestial Promise by Hayley Ann Solomon

Chasing Light by Patricia Glinton-Meicholas

China Suite and other poems by Gillian Bickley

For The Record And Other Poems Of Hong Kong by Gillian Bickley

Frida Kahlo's Cry And Other Poems by Laura Solomon

Heart to Heart: Poems by Patty Ho

Home, Away, Elsewhere by Vaughan Rapatahana

The Hummingbird Sometimes Flies Backwards by DJ Hamilton (Scheduled November 2019)

Immortelle and Bhandaaraa Poems by Lelawattee Manoo-Rahming.

In Vitro by Laura Solomon

Irreverent Poems For Pretentious People by Henrik Hoeg

The Layers Between by Celia Claase (*Collection of poems and essays*)

Life Lines by Shahilla Shariff

Moving House and Other Poems by Gillian Bickley

Of Leaves and Ashes by Patty Ho

Of Symbols Misused by Mary-Jane Newton

Over the Years by Gillian Bickley

Painting the Borrowed House: Poems by Kate Rogers

Perceptions by Gillian Bickley

Rain on the Pacific Coast by Elbert Siu Ping Lee

Refrain by Jason S Polley

Savage Charm by Ahmed Elbeshlawy

Shadow Play by James Norcliffe

Shadows in Deferment by Birgit Bunzel Linder

Shifting Sands by Deepa Vanjani

Sightings: a collection of Poetry by Gillian Bickley

Smoked Pearl by Akin Jeje

To Eastern Lands by Roger Uren

Unlocking by Mary-Jane Newton

Violet by Carolina Ilica

Wonder, Lust & Itchy Feet by Sally Dellow

The Year of the Apparitions by José Manuel Sevilla

INTERNATIONAL PROVERSE POETRY PRIZE ANTHOLOGIES

Mingled Voices ed Gillian and Verner Bickley

Mingled Voices 2 ed Gillian and Verner Bickley

Mingled Voices 3 ed Gillian and Verner Bickley

POETRY IN CHINESE

Moving House and Other Poems by Gillian Bickley (in Chinese with additional contents & b/w photographs)

EDUCATIONAL

(English Language)

Poems to Enjoy, Book 1 by Verner Bickley (3rd Ed) w. 1 audio CD (Graded poetry anthology w. teaching and learning notes, glossary, etc.)

Poems to Enjoy, Book 2 by Verner Bickley (3rd Ed) w. 2 audio CDs (Graded poetry anthology w. teaching and learning notes, glossary, etc.)

Poems to Enjoy, Book 3 by Verner Bickley (3rd Ed) w. 2 audio CDs (Graded poetry anthology w. teaching and learning notes, glossary, etc.)

Poems to Enjoy, Book 4 by Verner Bickley (3rd Ed) w. 2 audio CDs (Graded poetry anthology w. teaching and learning notes, glossary, etc.)

Poems to Enjoy, Book 5 by Verner Bickley (3rd Ed) w. 3 audio CDs (Graded poetry anthology w. teaching and learning notes, glossary, etc.)